SCHIRMER'S LIBRARY
OF MUSICAL CLASSICS

Vol. 2020

Scott Joplin

Complete Rags

For Piano

with an Introduction by Max Morath

ISBN 978-0-7935-6773-7

G. SCHIRMER, Inc.

DISTRIBUTED BY

HAL•LEONARD®
CORPORATION
7777 W. BLUEMOUND RD. P.O. BOX 13819 MILWAUKEE, WI 53213

CONTENTS

PREFACE

Ragtime is an *American* music. But having said this, one must add that while ragtime could have come to life only in America, it is truly a music distilled from the music of the whole world. Almost all the musical forms and traditions you can think of found their way here and were blended by black musical genius into this new form.

"Ragtime" is a quaint and surely inadequate term for this startling musical synthesis (a synthesis still in progress), for American music is no longer called "ragtime" or even "jazz." But although the labels change, the synthesizing continues, and the American musical melting pot continues to bubble.

Ragtime was the first synthesis and when it surfaced in the late 1890s, there was little understanding of the unique role America was to play in the musical world. "Popular" music was then a strange and suspicious concept and was, if not completely unnoticed, then certainly unaccepted by most of the musical and artistic intelligentsia. The idea that serious artists could be at work in this field was simply not considered. Along with the rest of "popular" music, rags were dismissed as impertinence or trash. It has taken many years for the nation to mellow and accept the best of ragtime and other early forms of native musical expression, both black and white, for what they are—*art*.

The consistent champion and pioneer spokesman in this acceptance has been Rudi Blesh. After years of dedicated study and impeccable research, he collaborated with the late Harriet Janis to write *They All Played Ragtime* (revised edition, Grove Press 1959). This marvelously readable book will always be the bedrock of ragtime biography and musicology. Blesh also wrote the introduction to the New York Public Library's 1971 publication, *The Collected Works of Scott Joplin*, edited by Vera Brodsky Lawrence. His research and evaluation in these two works supplies most of the biographical and publishing data offered in this collection, as indeed it must for all contemporary treatments of this subject.

Scott Joplin was born in Texarkana, probably on what is now the Arkansas side of the line, in 1868. His mother had been a freewoman since birth; his father, newly emancipated, had been a performing musician in his slave days.

In spite of poverty, the young Joplin had an early education in music and a reasonably serviceable upright piano for his eager practicing. But not too much is known of Joplin's early years. He is said to have left home at fourteen after a dispute with his father over his ambition for a career in music rather than trade.

His wanderings as an itinerant pianist and entertainer in the 1880s and '90s took him throughout the Midwest, with long stops in Chicago and St. Louis. During these *wanderjahre* Joplin absorbed the rich layers of music in that Mississippi Valley heartland, and, equipped with formal training acquired where and when he could find it, plus a rare mixture of inborn talent, classical discipline and folk understanding he developed his superb piano music. As Rudi Blesh wrote in his introduction to *The Collected Works of Scott Joplin*, Joplin "effected a basic and altogether remarkable fusion of Afro-American rhythm, American folk song both black and white, and the musical principles and procedures that America has traditionally derived from and shared with Europe."

In the late 1890s Joplin settled in Sedalia, Missouri—a tough rail-head town with a prosperous "district" and plenty of jobs for good players. He soon became the leader of the black musical community as well as a popular entertainer, and though still only in his late twenties, the sought-after mentor of younger player-composers. It was in Sedalia that the famous *Maple Leaf Rag* was first published by John Stark and Son, and where the outlines of other Joplin rags were first sketched.

The mirror image of Joplin's initials and those of his publisher John Stark has intrigued many who look for a mystical relationship between these two men of different races and divergent worlds, meeting in Sedalia in 1899 and making almost instant musical history with the publication of the *Maple Leaf Rag*. John Stark was not the first to publish ragtime; other rags were being published elsewhere including Joplin's first, *Original Rags*, issued by Carl Hoffman in Kansas City. But Stark brought total dedication to his publishing enterprise. The Stark imprint was a proud one; it heralded the classics in ragtime's otherwise teeming mediocrity. The tough but sensitive John Stark, nearing what would be called retirement age today, came to the publishing business as a novice. But for twenty years even until his death in 1927, he championed against all odds the publication of classic ragtime as art, as *music*, finally losing money but working away at it, printing the music exactly as his gifted composers penned it, loving the rags and promoting them with untiring zeal.

Backed by Stark, Joplin returned to St. Louis at World's Fair time, and in those first years of the new century that city teemed with action and ferment. Every ragtime player worth his salt hit town for the good money and eager crowds, and St. Louis established a reputation that is still acknowledged—the home of classic ragtime. During these crucial years Scott Joplin channeled his pent-up creativity into the precise style of the piano pieces published here.

Joplin, restless again, left St. Louis in 1907, moving first to Chicago and then to New York where his professional life quickened and his composing genius flowered anew. It was during these New York years that he devoted more and more time to his beloved project, the opera *Treemonisha*, a project doomed to failure, a failure that surely hastened his death.

Scott Joplin died in New York City on April 1, 1917, the week that America entered World War I. Sweeping changes were in store for the nation. Ragtime was already quaint, diluted by commercialism, ready to give way to that next exciting synthesis of American music to be called "jazz."

Joplin's music lay dormant for many years, cherished by a few collectors and relished by pianists lucky enough to stumble upon dog-eared original copies in a piano bench or music cabinet. But if Joplin was eclipsed for many years, it is incorrect to assume that he was unknown in his time. Scott Joplin was no feckless ascetic working against his time; he was very much of his time, recognized and respected by fellow musicians and known to a music-hungry public. If that public was unaware of the details of his life, if it did not follow his tortured career to its tragic finale in a charity hospital on Wards Island; if indeed it had forgotten or never known that this gifted artist was a black man trapped in prejudice and circumstance, it did know his music. *Maple Leaf Rag* may be the single most successful composition in the history of popular music—a piece that influenced every composer and pianist for many years and which established the form and content of classic piano ragtime during its startling sweep of public acceptance at the turn of the century.

John Stark, upon learning of Joplin's death, pronounced an obituary succinct and all-encompassing: "Scott Joplin is dead. A homeless itinerant, he left his mark on American music."

—MAX MORATH

G. Schirmer is pleased to present this complete new edition of the Scott Joplin piano rags. In an attempt to improve upon older editions, we have re-engraved all of the pieces; to facilitate performance and reduce page turns, we have designed the layout so that repeating sections appear on facing pages. The music has been carefully edited to remove mistakes from prior publications.

We are confident that this significant addition to the Schirmer Library will help ensure the enduring popularity of these wonderful pieces.

ORIGINAL RAGS

* Picked by Scott Joplin
1899
arranged by Charles N. Daniels

* "Pick," in 1899, was a slang term for playing ragtime piano; Daniels was a staff arranger at the
original publisher, and undoubtedly had little or nothing to do with the composition of this piece.

Fine

MAPLE LEAF RAG

Tempo di marcia

Trio

Fine

PEACHERINE RAG

1901

Not too fast

Fine

THE EASY WINNERS
A Ragtime Two-step

Introduction
Not fast

1901

Fine

A BREEZE FROM ALABAMA
March and Two-step

1902

Fine

ELITE SYNCOPATIONS

Introduction
Not fast

1902

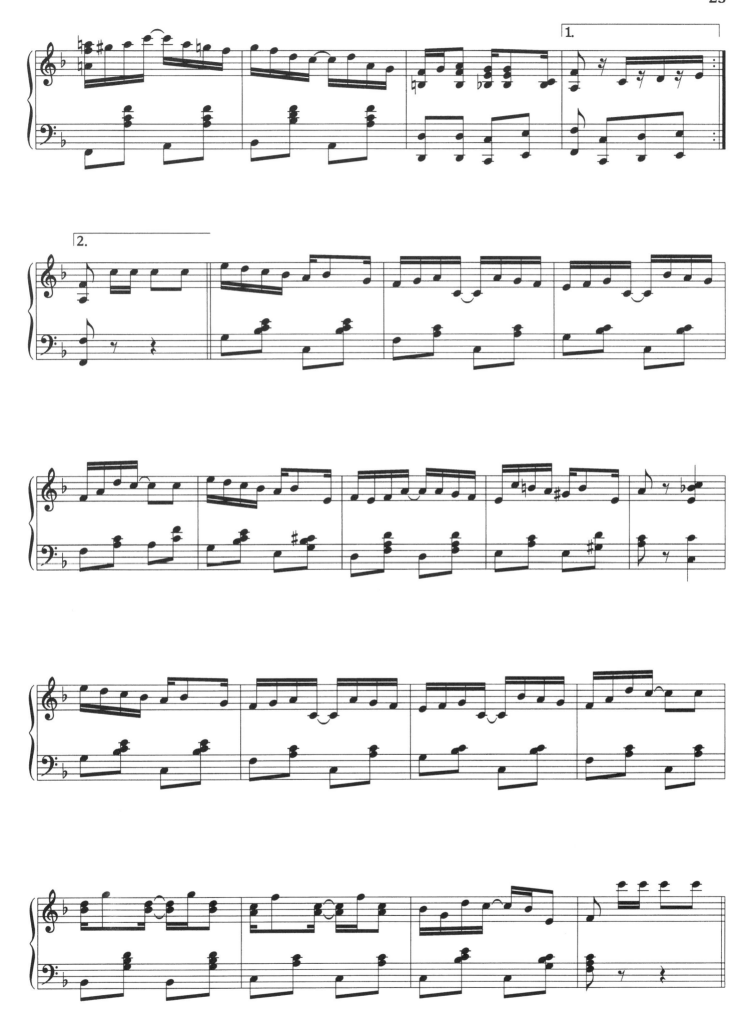

Fine

Dedicated to James Brown and his Mandolin Club

THE ENTERTAINER
A Ragtime Two-step

Introduction
Not fast

1902

repeat R.H. 8va higher

Fine

THE STRENUOUS LIFE
A Ragtime Two-step

1902

39

Fine

WEEPING WILLOW
A Ragtime Two-step

1903

Not fast

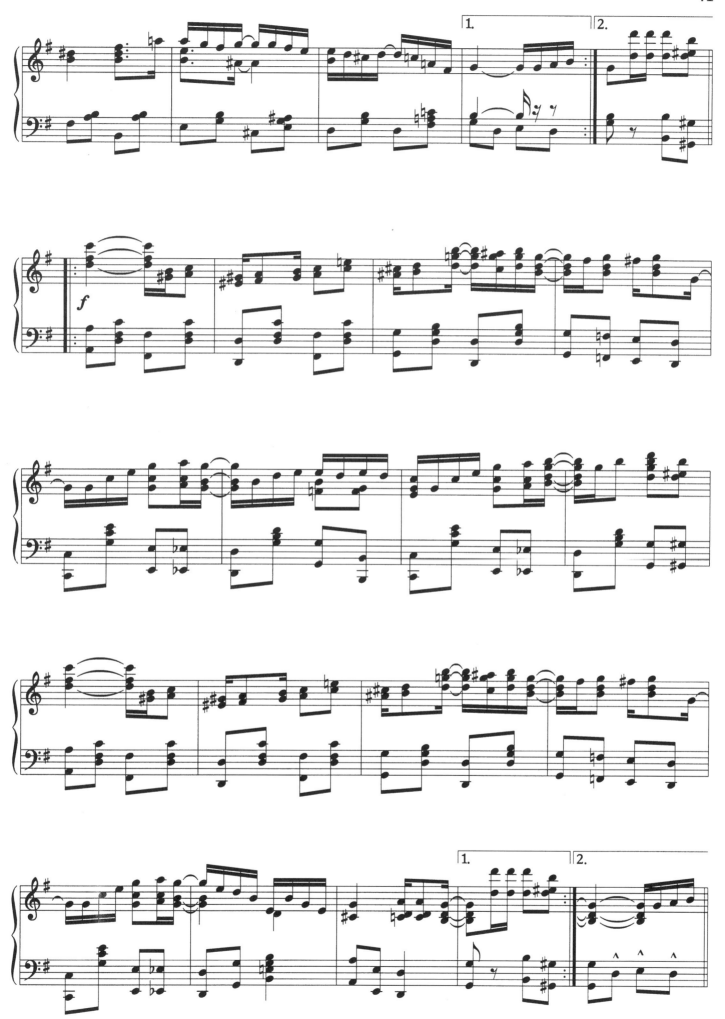

Fine

PALM LEAF RAG

1903

Play a little slow

Fine

THE FAVORITE
A Ragtime Two-step

Introduction
Slow march tempo

1904

50

Fine

THE SYCAMORE
A Concert Rag

1904

Tempo di marcia

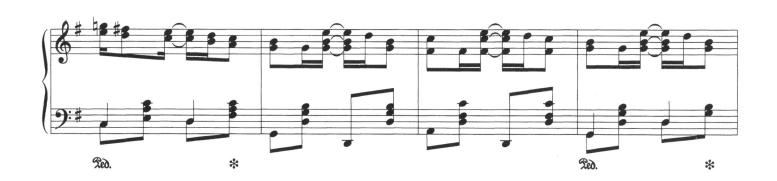

Fine

THE CASCADES
A Rag

1904

Tempo di marcia

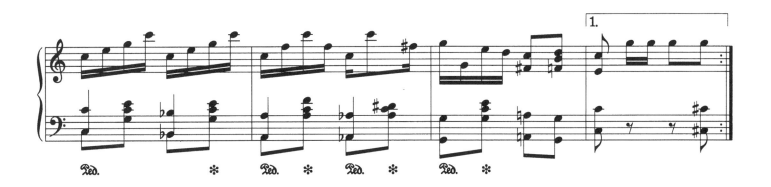

Fine

THE CHRYSANTHEMUM
An African-American Intermezzo

Introduction
Slow march tempo

1904

Fine

Respectfully dedicated to Miss Minnie Wade

LEOLA
Two-step

1905

Slow march tempo

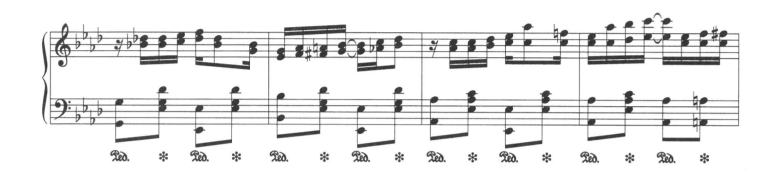

Fine

EUGENIA

Notice! Don't play this piece fast. It is never right to play "ragtime" fast.
—Author

1905

Slow march tempo ♩ = 72

Fine

RAG TIME DANCE
A Stop-time Two-step

1906

Not too fast

NOTICE: To get the desired effect of "stop-time," the pianist will please *stamp* the heel of one foot heavily upon the floor at the word "Stamp." Do not raise the toe from the floor while stamping.

Stamp   Stamp   Stamp   Stamp   Stamp   Stamp   Stamp   Stamp

Stamp   Stamp   Stamp   Stamp   Stamp   Stamp   Stamp   Stamp

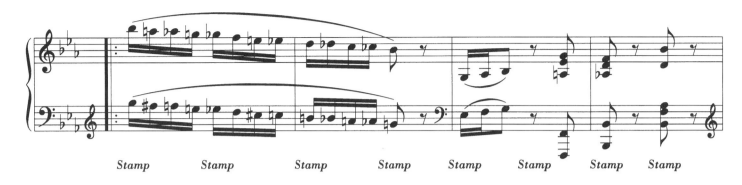

Stamp · Stamp · Stamp · Stamp · Stamp · Stamp · Stamp · Stamp

Stamp · Stamp · Stamp · Stamp · Stamp · Stamp · Stamp · Stamp

Stamp · Stamp · Stamp · Stamp · Stamp · Stamp · Stamp · Stamp

Stamp · Stamp · Stamp · Stamp · Stamp · Stamp · Stamp · Stamp

Stamp · Stamp · Stamp · Stamp · Stamp · Stamp · Stamp · Stamp

Fine

GLADIOLUS RAG

Notice! Don't play this piece fast. It
is never right to play "ragtime" fast.
—Author

Slow march tempo

1907

Fine

Respectfully dedicated to Miss Mildred Ponder

THE NONPAREIL
A Rag & Two-step

1907

Notice! Don't play this piece fast. It
is never right to play "ragtime" fast.
　　　　　　　　—Author

Slow march tempo

Fine

Notice! Don't play this piece fast. It
is never right to play "ragtime" fast.
—Author

ROSE LEAF RAG
A Ragtime Two-step

1907

Slow march tempo

Fine

SEARCH-LIGHT RAG

Notice! Do not play this piece fast.
It is never right to play "ragtime" fast.
—Author

1907

Slow march tempo

Fine

FIG LEAF
A High-class Rag

Notice! Don't play this piece fast. It
is never right to play "ragtime" fast.
     —Author

1908

Slow march tempo

Fine

SUGAR CANE
A Ragtime Two-step

Notice! Don't play this piece fast. It
is never right to play "ragtime" fast.
—Author

Slow march tempo

♩ = 100

1908

Fine

Respectfully dedicated to the Five Musical Spillers

PINE APPLE RAG

Notice! Don't play this piece fast. It
is never right to play "ragtime" fast.
— Author

1908

Slow march tempo ♩ = 100

Fine

WALL STREET RAG

Notice! Don't play this piece fast.
It is never right to play "ragtime" fast.
—Author

1909

Very slow march time

Panic in Wall Street, brokers feeling melancholy.

Good times coming.

112

Good times have come.

Listening to the strains of genuine Negro ragtime, brokers forget their cares.

Fine

PLEASANT MOMENTS
Ragtime Waltz

1909

Slow waltz time

Fine

COUNTRY CLUB
Ragtime Two-step

1909

Notice! Don't play this piece fast. It
is never right to play "ragtime" fast.
—Author

Slow march time

Fine

EUPHONIC SOUNDS

Notice! Don't play this piece fast.
It is never right to play "ragtime" fast.
—Author

1909

Slow march time

Fine

Notice! Don't play this piece fast. It
is never right to play "ragtime" fast.
—Author

Respectfully dedicated to the C.V.B.A.

PARAGON RAG

1909

Slow march time

Trio

Fine

STOPTIME RAG

To get the desired effect of "Stop-Time," the pianist should *stamp* the heel of one foot
heavily upon the floor at the word "Stamp." Do not raise the toe from the floor while stamping.

1910

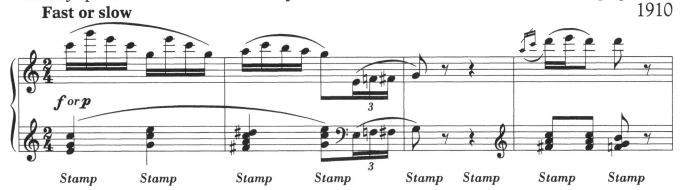

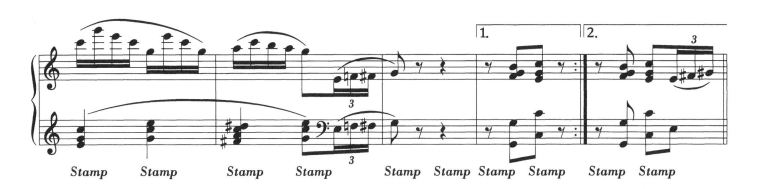

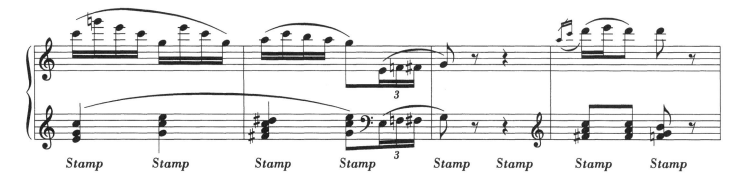

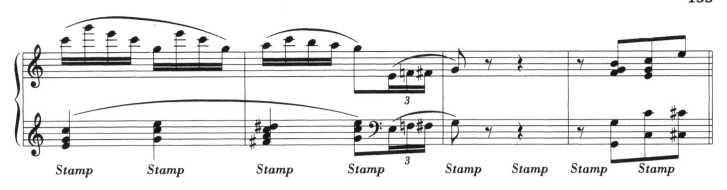

Stamp   Stamp   Stamp   Stamp   Stamp   Stamp   Stamp   Stamp

Stamp   Stamp   Stamp   Stamp   Stamp   Stamp   Stamp   Stamp

Stamp   Stamp   Stamp   Stamp   Stamp   Stamp   Stamp   Stamp

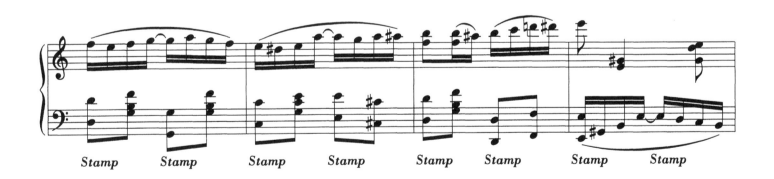

Stamp   Stamp   Stamp   Stamp   Stamp   Stamp   Stamp   Stamp

Stamp   Stamp   Stamp   Stamp   Stamp   Stamp   Stamp   Stamp   Stamp   Stamp

Stamp   Stamp   Stamp Stamp   Stamp   Stamp   Stamp Stamp   Stamp   Stamp

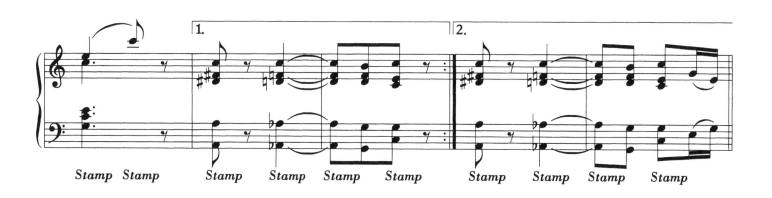

Stamp Stamp   Stamp   Stamp   Stamp   Stamp   Stamp   Stamp   Stamp   Stamp

Stamp   Stamp   Stamp   Stamp   Stamp   Stamp   Stamp   Stamp

Stamp   Stamp   Stamp   Stamp   Stamp   Stamp   Stamp   Stamp

Stamp   Stamp   Stamp   Stamp   Stamp Stamp   Stamp   Stamp   Stamp   Stamp

Stamp   Stamp   Stamp   Stamp   Stamp   Stamp   Stamp   Stamp

Stamp   Stamp   Stamp   Stamp   Stamp   Stamp   Stamp   Stamp

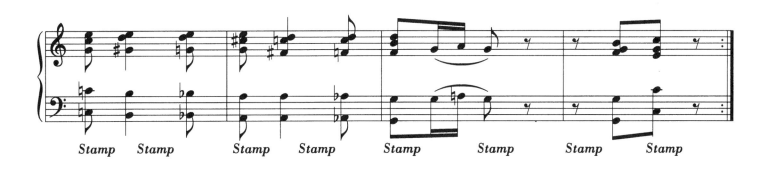

Stamp   Stamp   Stamp   Stamp   Stamp   Stamp   Stamp   Stamp

Stamp   Stamp   Stamp   Stamp   Stamp   Stamp   Stamp   Stamp

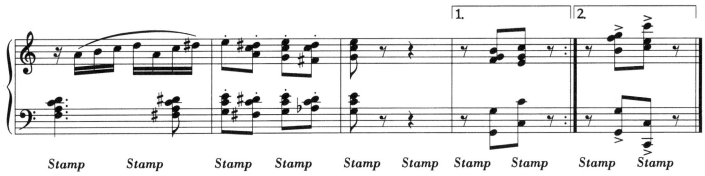

Stamp   Stamp   Stamp   Stamp   Stamp   Stamp   Stamp   Stamp   Stamp   Stamp

Fine

SCOTT JOPLIN'S NEW RAG

1912

Allegro moderato

Coda

Fine

MAGNETIC RAG

1914

Allegretto ma non troppo

Fine

REFLECTION RAG

(Syncopated Musings)

1917

Slow march tempo

f sempre

Fine

SWIPESY
Cakewalk

Scott Joplin
and
Arthur Marshall
1900

Slow

Fine

SUN FLOWER SLOW DRAG
Rag Time Two-step

Scott Joplin
and
Scott Hayden
1901

Introduction
Not fast

Fine

SOMETHING DOING
A Ragtime Two-step

Scott Joplin
and
Scott Hayden
1903

Introduction
Not fast

* This chord may be $\begin{array}{c}\text{♮} \\ \text{♮}\end{array}$ as it is earlier.

Fine

LILY QUEEN
A Ragtime Two-step

Scott Joplin
and
Arthur Marshall
1907

Notice! Don't play this piece fast. It
is never right to play "ragtime" fast.
—Authors

Moderato

Fine

HELIOTROPE BOUQUET
A Slow Drag Two-step

Scott Joplin
and
Louis Chauvin
1907

Notice! Don't play this piece fast. It
is never right to play "ragtime" fast.
—Authors

Slow march tempo

Fine

FELICITY RAG
A Ragtime Two-step

Scott Joplin
and
Scott Hayden
1911

Tempo di marcia

Fine

KISMET RAG

Scott Joplin
and
Scott Hayden
1913

Introduction
Not fast

Fine

BETHENA
A Concert Waltz

1905

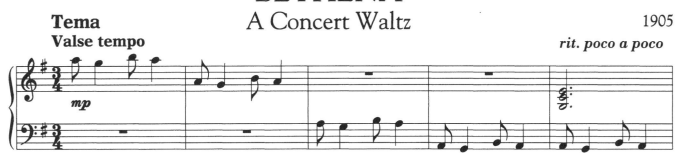

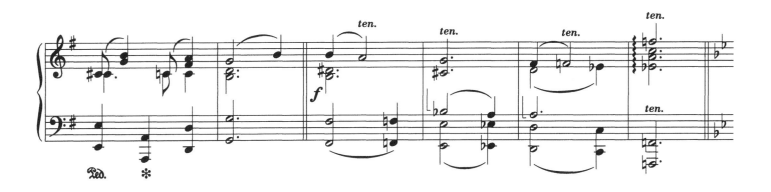

Finale

Fine

SOLACE
A Mexican Serenade

1909

Very slow march time

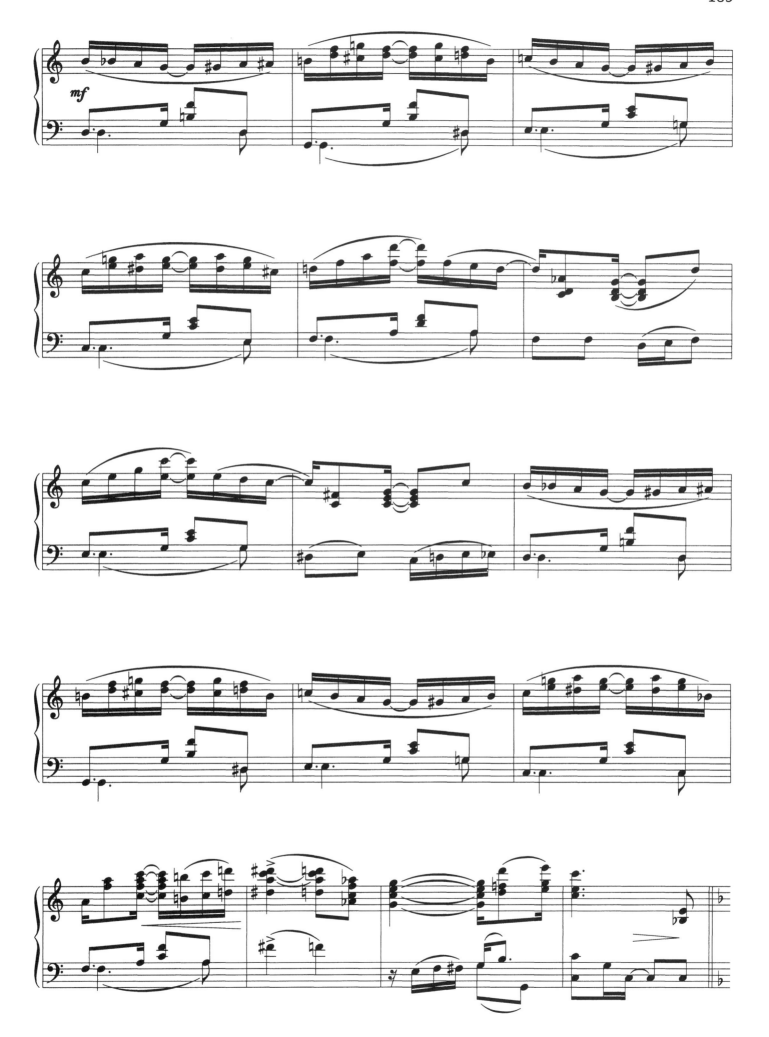

Fine

SCHOOL OF RAGTIME

6 EXERCISES FOR PIANO
BY
SCOTT JOPLIN
Composer of *Maple Leaf Rag*

REMARKS

What is scurrilously called ragtime is an invention that is here to stay. That is now conceded by all classes of musicians. That all publications masquerading under the name of ragtime are not the genuine article will be better known when these exercises are studied. That real ragtime of the higher class is rather difficult to play is a painful truth which most pianists have discovered. Syncopations are no indication of light or trashy music, and to shy bricks* at "hateful ragtime" no longer passes for musical culture. To assist amateur players in giving the "Joplin Rags" that weird and intoxicating effect intended by the composer is the object of this work.

EXERCISE NO. 1

It is evident that, by giving each note its proper time and by scrupulously observing the ties, you will get the effect. So many are careless in these respects that we will specify each feature. In this number, strike the first note and hold it through the time belonging to the second note. The upper staff is not syncopated, and is not to be played. The perpendicular dotted lines running from the syncopated note below to the two notes above will show exactly its duration. Play slowly until you catch the swing, and never play ragtime fast at any time.

Slow march tempo (*Count Two*)

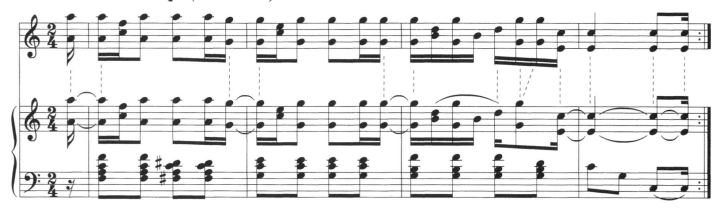

* To hurl insults.

EXERCISE NO. 2

This style is rather more difficult, especially for those who are careless with the left hand, and are prone to vamp.* The first note should be given the full length of three sixteenths, and no more. The second note is struck in its proper place and the third note is not struck but is joined with the second as though they were one note. This treatment is continued to the end of the exercise.

Slow march tempo *(Count Two)*

EXERCISE NO. 3

This style is very effective when neatly played. If you have observed the object of the dotted lines they will lead you to a proper rendering of this number and you will find it interesting.

Slow march tempo *(Count Two)*

* To improvise an accompaniment, especially rhythmically.

EXERCISE NO. 4

The fourth and fifth notes here form one tone, and also in the middle of the second measure and so to the end. You will observe that it is a syncopation only when the tied notes are on the same degree of the staff. Slurs indicate a legato movement.

Slow march tempo *(Count Two)*

EXERCISE NO. 5

The first ragtime effect here is the second note, right hand, but instead of two sixteenths with a tie, it is an eighth note. In the last part of this measure, the tie is used because the tone is carried across the bar. This is a pretty style and not as difficult as it seems on first trial.

Slow march tempo *(Count Two)*

EXERCISE NO. 6

The instructions given, together with the dotted lines, will enable you to interpret this variety which has very pleasing effects. We wish to say here that the "Joplin ragtime" is destroyed by careless or imperfect rendering, and very often good players lose the effect entirely, by playing too fast. They are harmonized with the supposition that each note will be played as it is written, as it takes this and also the proper time divisions to complete the sense intended.

Slow march tempo *(Count Two)*